# THEATR Y
# SHERMAN
# THEATRE

Royal
**Exchange**
Theatre

the bruntwood
prize for playwriting 2013
in partnership with the Royal Exchange Theatre

Winner

# BIRD

## Katherine Chandler

*Bird* is              Theatre
co-producti            man Theatre,
Cardiff, on 1          ' to the Royal
    Excl                016.

D1382216

# BIRD

## Katherine Chandler

## Cast

| | |
|---|---|
| AVA | Georgia Henshaw |
| CLAIRE | Siwan Morris |
| DAN | Connor Allen |
| LEE | Guy Rhys |
| TASH | Rosie Sheehy |

## Creative Team

| | |
|---|---|
| Director | Rachel O'Riordan |
| Designer | Kenny Miller |
| Lighting Designer | Kevin Treacy |
| Composer and Sound Designer | Simon Slater |
| Assistant Director | Elgan Rhys |
| Deputy Stage Manager | Charlotte Unwin |
| Head of Wardrobe | Deryn Tudor |
| Casting Director | Sophie Parrott CDG |
| Fight Director | Kev McCurdy |
| Vocal Coach | Patricia Logue |

## Director's Note

Katherine Chandler, the Sherman's Playwright-in-Residence, received the Judges Award in the 2013 Bruntwood Prize for Playwriting for *Bird*, so I am delighted that the Sherman is now presenting this production with the Royal Exchange Theatre.

*Bird* is a play that achieves something vital. It puts the voices of vulnerable young women at the centre of the narrative. It makes us, as the audience, acknowledge that we allow the disadvantaged young to be ignored, marginalised and disregarded. *Bird* makes us listen. *Bird* asks us to think. I am proud to be producing this play with the Royal Exchange Theatre as we try to keep the stories of those who live on the margins of a safe society, front and centre.

*Rachel O'Riordan*
*May 2016*

# Creatives

### Katherine Chandler (Author)

Katherine is an award-winning writer working in theatre, film and television. Katherine was awarded the inaugural Wales Drama Award by the BBC and National Theatre Wales and won the judges prize in the 2013 Bruntwood Prize for Playwriting with *Bird*.

Twice a finalist for the prestigious Susan Smith Blackburn Prize with her plays *Before It Rains* and *Parallel Lines*, Katherine also won the Writers Guild Playwright Award at the 2013 Theatre Critics of Wales Awards.

Her most recent works have been produced by companies such as BBC Drama, Clean Break, National Theatre Wales, National Theatre Connections, Dirty Protest, Sherman Cymru, Bristol Old Vic and Manchester Royal Exchange Theatre.

Currently Katherine is working on a variety of exciting commissions with companies such as BBC Drama, National Theatre Wales, Sherman Theatre, Clean Break and Theatre Clwyd.

### Rachel O'Riordan (Director)

Rachel is the Artistic Director of the Sherman Theatre, for whom she has directed *Bird, Iphigenia in Splott* (Best New Play at the UK Theatre Awards 2015, first Welsh theatre production to transfer straight to the National Theatre), *The Lion, The Witch and The Wardrobe, A Doll's House, Romeo and Juliet, Arabian Nights* and Sherman Cymru's co-production with Òran Mór A Play, A Pie and A Pint: *Leviathan*.

Before joining the Sherman, she was Artistic Director at Perth Theatre where work included: *Macbeth* (Perth/Tron); *The Seafarer* (Perth/Lyric); *The Odd Couple* (Female Version); *Moonlight and Magnolias; Someone Who'll Watch Over Me and Twelfth Night.*

Other work includes: *Unfaithful* (Traverse); *The Absence of Women* (Tricycle); *Hurricane* (West End/59E59 Off-Broadway); *Everything is Illuminated* (Hampstead); *Miss Julie, Animal Farm* (Peter Hall Company, Theatre Royal); *Absolution* (Guna Nua/First Irish NY); *Much Ado About Nothing; The Glass Menagerie, Merry Christmas Betty Ford* (Lyric, Belfast); *A Christmas Carol, Gates of Gold, Grimm Tales* (Library, Manchester); *Over the Bridge* (Green Shoot/Waterfront Hall, Belfast); *Elizabeth – Almost By Chance a Woman* (Kabosh/Project, Dublin*); Protestants* (Soho); *Arguments for Terrorism, Cold Turkey at Nana's* (Òran Mór).

Rachel founded and was Artistic Director of Ransom, Belfast, for whom she commissioned, developed and directed new work. Ransom's work toured extensively across the UK and Ireland.

Awards include Best Director and Best Ensemble for *The Seafarer* (2013 Critics' Award for Theatre in Scotland); Best Director *for Absolution* (First Irish Theatre Festival Awards, New York, 2010). She has been nominated three times for Best Director at the UK Theatre Awards.

### Kenny Miller (Designer)

Kenny Miller is a freelance designer and director who was for many years Head of Design/Associate Director at the Citizens' Theatre, Glasgow, and is currently Associate Artist: Designer for the Sherman Theatre, Cymru.

He has worked in theatre and opera both nationally and internationally, designing and directing for many companies such as: Royal Court Theatre, London; Royal Shakespeare Company; Oxford Stage Company; Hampstead Theatre; Theatre Royal Stratford East; Palace Theatre Watford; Greenwich Theatre; Bush Theatre; Donmar

Warehouse; Lyceum Theatre, Edinburgh; Oldham Coliseum Theatre; Tron Theatre and Dundee Rep Theatre.

He has won three Critics' Awards for Theatre in Scotland for: *Scrooge* (Best Production), *Smoking With Lulu* (Best Technical), and *A Little Bit of Ruff* (Best Ensemble). He has also won the Manchester Evening News Award for *10 Rillington Place* (Best Designed Production).

### Kevin Treacy (Lighting Designer)

Designs include: *Romeo and Juliet, Arabian Nights, A Doll's House* and *The Lion, The Witch and The Wardrobe* (Sherman Cymru); *Unfaithful* (Traverse, Edinburgh); *The Government Inspector* and *Arrah-na-Pogue* (Abbey Theatre, Dublin); *Twelfth Night* (Nottingham Playhouse); *Beside the Sea* (Southbank Centre); *The Seafarer* (Perth Theatre and Lyric, Belfast); *Macbeth* (Perth/Tron, Glasgow); *Blithe Spirit* (Perth); *The Nose* (The Performance Corporation).

Irish Times Award for Best Lighting Design. Opera designs include: *The Turn of the Screw* (Buxton Opera and Kolobov Novaya, Moscow); *Faramondo* (Handel Festspiele, Göttingen); *La Bohéme, Carmen* (Nevill Holt*); Imeneo, Rodelinda* (Royal College of Music*); Macbeth* (Welsh National Opera).

### Simon Slater (Composer and Sound Designer)

Theatre includes: *A Doll's House, Arabian Nights* (Sherman Cymru); *Before It Rains* (Sherman Cymru/Bristol Old Vic); *The Winter's Tale* (Sam Wanamaker, Globe, London); *'Tis Pity She's a Whore* (Globe, London); *Untold Stories* (Watermill*); My Mother Said I Never Should* (St James); *Talking Heads* (Bath Theatre Royal); *Carmen Disruption* (Almeida); *Constellations* (Duke of York's/Royal Court/New York); *Great Expectations* (Vaudeville); *Ghosts* (New Vic, Stoke); *Single Spies* (The Rose, Kingston); *Wonderland, Raving, No Naughty Bits, Enlightenment* (Hampstead); *Land of our Fathers, Handful of Stars* (Trafalgar Studios/Theatre503); *Cannibals* (Royal Exchange Theatre); *The Lady in the Van* (national tour*); The Deep Blue Sea, Death of a Salesman, The Grouch, As You Like It, Wind in the Willows* (West Yorkshire Playhouse); *Henry V, Julius Caesar, Romeo and Juliet* (Royal Shakespeare Company*); Macbeth* (Albery, West End); *Rose Rage* (Chicago Shakespeare Theatre/Duke's Theatre New York).

### Elgan Rhys (Assistant Director)

Elgan's previous Associate Director credits include *Blue/Orange* (Canoe Theatre); *Woyzeck* and *Dan Y Wenallt/Under Milk Wood* (University of South Wales). His previous Assistant Director credits are *Yuri* (August 012); *After The End* (Dirty Protest); and *Sherman Swingers* (Sherman Cymru).

Other credits include: *Ti.Me, Llais/Voice* (co-deviser with Cwmni Pluen), *Follow Me/Dilyn Fi* (deviser/performer with Cwmni'r Frân Wen); *Fi a Miss World* (writer with S4C/It's My Shout). Elgan is the co-founder and co-director for Cwmni Pluen; a company that strives to create original, challenging and unconventional work. Cwmni Pluen is the Sherman Theatre's first ever company in residence.

### Sophie Parrott CDG (Casting Director)

Theatre includes: *My Mother Said I Never Should* (St James); *Yen* (Royal Court/Royal Exchange Theatre); *Britannia Waves the Rules* (Royal Exchange Theatre/tour); *Pomona* (additional casting for National Theatre Shed/Royal Exchange, Manchester); *A Midsummer Night's Dream* (Liverpool Everyman*); The Crocodile* (Manchester International Festival); *Billy Liar* (Royal Exchange Theatre).

Television includes (as Casting Director): *Doctors*; (as Casting Associate): *Thirteen, Call the Midwife Series IV and V, The Bletchley Circle II, Silent Witness XVII and XVIII*.

# Cast

### Georgia Henshaw (Ava)

Georgia has appeared in numerous television shows including; *Bedlam, Being Human, Casualty, Doctors, EastEnders, Holby City, Missing, Shelfstackers, The Coroner, The Crash, Two Pints of Lager and a Packet of Crisps, Waterloo Road* (BBC); *DCI Banks, Moving Wallpaper, The Bill, The Children, Law & UK, Renaissance* (ITV); *Banana & Cucumber, Skins* (E4), *Trollied* (Sky).

Her first film role was as Rosie Barnes in *Angus, Thongs, and Full Frontal Snogging* (Paramount Pictures); Julian Kerridge's *Seamonsters, In the Dark Half* (Cinema Six); *The Hatching* (released in America through Lionsgate Studios); *Peep Dish;* (Darragh Mortell); *Blind Eye, Between You and Me* (Digital Shorts); *Emily Goes to Pimlico* (Pimlico Films).

### Rosie Sheehy (Tash)

Rosie graduated from RADA in July 2015 and stepped straight into a leading role in *Chicken* for Paines Plough which forms part of their Roundabout season at the Edinburgh Fringe Festival. She was last seen on stage at The Old Vic opposite Bertie Carvel in *The Hairy Ape* directed by Richard Jones.

### Siwan Morris (Claire)

Siwan's television credits include: *Caedydd* (series 1-4), *Casualty, Gwaith Cartref* (series regular – Fiction Factory), *Doctors, Doctor Who, Holby City, Our Girl, Tales of Pleasure Beach, The Bench, Wolfblood, Whites* (series 1–3) (BBC); *Antigone, Belonging, Social Action* (BBC Wales); *Pishyn Glo, Y Streic A Fi* (S4C); *Can Passionata, Con Passionate* (Apollo TV); *Miss Marple, Mine All Mine* (ITV); *Skins* (series 1–2) (Channel 4/E4); *20 Things to do Before You're 30* (Tiger Aspect); *The Bill* (Talkback Thames) *The Marvellous Handshake* (Satellite Productions); *Mind to Kill* (Fiction Factory/HTV; *Sister Lulu* (Gaucho/Channel 4).

Theatre credits include: *Violence and Son* (Royal Court); *Tonypandemonium, A Good Night Out in the Valleys* (National Theatre Wales); *Knives in Hens* (Bath Theatre Royal); *A Midsummer Night's Dream, Suddenly Last Summer, King Lear, The Rabbit, Flora's War, Hosts of Rebecca, Rape of the Fair Country, The Journey of Mary Kelly* (Clwyd Theatre); *The Seagull* (Bristol Old Vic); *Much Ado About Nothing* (UK tour), *The Merchant of Venice, The Winter's Tale* (Ludlow Theatre Festival); *Feast of Snails* (Lyric); *Gas Station Angel* (Fiction Factory/Royal Court).

Film credits include: *Dark Signal* (Dark Signal Ltd); *The Machine* (Pandora Films).

Radio credits include: *Summer is Long to Come, Dylan Thomas Shorts, The True Memoirs of Harriette Wilson* (BBC); *Dover and the Unkindest Cut of All, On Top of the World* (Radio 4); *Same as it Ever Was* (Fiction Factory); *Station Road* (BBC Radio Drama).

### Guy Rhys (Lee)

Guy trained at the Drama Centre. Theatre includes: *Pomona* (Orange Tree/National Theatre/Royal Exchange Theatre); *My Father, Odysseus* (Unicorn); *Wendy & Peter Pan* (Royal Shakespeare Company); *Star Cross'd* (Oldham Coliseum); *A View From the Bridge* (Royal Exchange Theatre); *Rafta Rafta* (Bolton Octagon/New Vic); *Mother Courage and Her Children, The Powerbook* (National Theatre); *The Allotment* (New Perspectives); *A Streetcar Named Desire* (Theatr Clywd); *Murmuring Judges* (Birmingham Rep); *Hijra* (West Yorkshire Playhouse); *Romeo and Juliet* (Chichester Festival Theatre); *The Ramayana* (Birmingham Rep/National Theatre).

Television includes: *The Crimson Field, Emmerdale, Fallout, Sorted, Doctors, Holby City, No Angels, The Last Detective, Outlaws, Fat Friends, Dalziel & Pascoe, A&E, Big Bad World Ii, The Bill.*

**Connor Allen (Dan)**
Since graduating from Trinity St David as an actor, Connor has worked with prominent welsh companies such as National Theatre Wales's *Stories of the Streets*, Taking Flight Theatre Company's, *Real Human Being* and Mess Up The Mess's *Hidden*. He was also the Winner of Triforce's Monologue Slam, taking part in the London Winner's Edition representing Wales. Television work includes Jason in *Our Girl* for BBC Wales.

*Bird* in rehearsal

Georgia
Henshaw

Rosie Sheehy

Katherine
Chandler

Rachel
O'Riordan

Connor Allen

Guy Rhys

Siwan Morris

Photography by Kirsten McTernan

# THEATR Y SHERMAN THEATRE

## About the Sherman

The Sherman is one of the UK's leading producing houses, making and curating exciting theatre for audiences and developing meaningful partnerships with the best of UK and international companies. With a focus on the development and presentation of new writing in both English and Welsh, the Sherman supports and nurtures emerging artists.

Citizens of Cardiff and beyond are able to connect with the theatre through a relevant, inspiring and visionary Creative Learning programme. The Paul Hamlyn Foundation funded project, Sherman 5, brings audiences into the theatre for the first time who have previously faced barriers to attendance.

In 2016 the Sherman became the first Welsh theatre to transfer to the National Theatre with the production of *Iphigenia in Splott*. The piece also received the UK Theatre Award for Best New Play 2015.

**029 2064 6900**
**shermancymru.co.uk**

Sherman Theatre acknowledges the support of:
**Arts Council Wales**
**BIG Lottery**
**British Council**
**JMK Trust**
**Paul Hamlyn Foundation**
**The Richard Carne Trust**

# Staff List

Situated in the heart of Manchester, the Royal Exchange Theatre is one of the UK's leading producing theatres. Its ambitious programme is inspired by the world's greatest stories: stories that have the power to change the way we see the world. That means taking artistic risks, working as part of exciting partnerships, championing new talent and seeking out bold collaborations. A record number of people experienced their work in the last year, and they continue to broaden their output on and offstage, to speak to the most diverse audiences in Manchester and beyond.

The Royal Exchange is committed to supporting and developing new writing. The Bruntwood Prize for Playwriting in partnership with the Royal Exchange Theatre is the UK's biggest playwriting competition and celebrated its 10th anniversary last year when the 2015 Prize was awarded to Katherine Soper for her play *Wish List*. This year also saw a successful co-production with the Royal Court Theatre of 2013 Bruntwood Prize Winner *Yen*.

To find out more please visit royalexchange.co.uk,
or follow us twitter.com/rxtheatre
facebook: royalexchangetheatre
Box Office 0161 833 9833

 **AGMA** ASSOCIATION OF GREATER MANCHESTER AUTHORITIES

 MANCHESTER CITY COUNCIL

 Supported using public funding by **ARTS COUNCIL ENGLAND** | LOTTERY FUNDED

Registered Charity Number 255424

# ROYAL EXCHANGE THEATRE STAFF

# DONORS, SUPPORTERS AND BENEFACTORS

## PRINCIPAL FUNDERS

## MAJOR SPONSORS

CHEETHAM BELL

## PROJECT SUPPORTERS

Addleshaw Goddard
The Andrew Lloyd Webber
   Foundation
The BBC Performing Arts
   Fund
Beaverbrooks Charitable
   Trust
Arnold & Brenda Bradshaw
The Co-operative
   Foundation
Computeam
Duchy of Lancaster
   Benevolent Fund
Garfield Weston Foundation
The Granada Foundation
Equity Charitable Trust –
The John Fernald Award
The J Paul Getty Jnr
   Charitable Trust
The John Thaw Foundation
The Madeleine Mabey Trust
Manchester Guardian
   Society
The Noël Coward
   Foundation
The Oglesby Charitable
   Trust
Ordinary People, Interesting
   Lives
The Paul Hamlyn
   Foundation
The Peter Henriques
   Memorial Fund
The PWC Foundation
The Raffle family
The Rayne Foundation
The Rycroft Childrens' Fund
Schroder Charitable Trust

Susan Hodgkiss CBE
Martyn & Valerie Torevell
We are AD

## PRINCIPAL MEMBERSHIP

Bruntwood
Cheetham Bell
Edmundson Electrical
Manchester Airport Group
   Regatta
Neil Eckersley Productions

## ENCORE MEMBERSHIP

Dewhurst Torevell
M.A.C Cosmetics

## ASSOCIATE MEMBERSHIP

Acies Group
Addleshaw Goddard
Atticus Legal
Beaverbrooks
Cargill Plc
Cityco
Computeam
Crowe Clark Whitehill
Galloways Printers
Grant Thornton
HFL Building Solutions
Hollins Strategic Land
MCS (International) Limited
Mills & Reeve
Pinsent Masons
RSM
Sanderson Weatherall
Sapphire Systems
Smart Alex
Whitebirk Finance Ltd

## PATRONS £1000+ PA

Phil & Julie Adams
Simon & Shalni Arora
Arnold & Brenda Bradshaw
Ben & Maggie Caldwell
Maureen Casket
Meg Cooper
Stephen & Helen Critchlow
Barbara Crossley
Amanda Fairclough
Brendan & Ellen Flood
Nick & Lesley Hopkinson
Richard & Elaine Johnson
William & Ariel Lees-Jones
Stuart Lees &
   Sue Tebby-Lees
Sandy Lindsay
Stuart Montgomery
Chris & Anne Morris
Christine Ovens
Stephen & Judy Poster
Raj & Reshma Ruia

UK Together
& all our anonymous
   patrons

## PLATINUM MEMBERSHIP

Chris & Sue Bangs
Angela Brookes
Professor R A Burchell
John & Penny Early
Peter & Judy Folkman
Samantha Rollason
Martin & Sandra Stone
Robin & Mary Taylor
Helen & Phil Wiles

## CATALYST DONORS

Anonymous
Roy Beckett
Sir Robert &
   Mrs Meriel Boyd
Bernard & Julie De Sousa
John & Penny Early
The Friends
Martin Harrison &
   Frances Hendrix
Eve & Peter Keeling
Chris & Mike Potter
Dr J L Pearsall
Jennifer Raffle
Martyn & Valerie Torevell
Gerry & Joanne Yeung

## REGULAR GIVING MEMBERS

Gold Membership £240+pa
G W Ball
Mr J Bishop & Mr J Taylor
Gary Buttriss-Holt
Mr E Cameron
Ronald Cassidy
Mr Peter Cooper
Mr P J Craven
Mrs Valerie Dunne
Rosalind Emsley-Smith
Mrs V Fletcher
James Garbett
Irene Gray
Mrs L Hawkins
George Ian Hood
Patricia Rose Kelly
Gillian & Kieron Lonergan
Sheila Malone
Jon Mason
Mr Donald Mather
Mr & Mrs Meldrum
Mr G M Morton
Pannone LLP
Mr & Mrs Rose
Sandra Thomas
Mr J D Wignall

"It is easy to lose faith in an over subscribed industry that has very little funding to support new work, but the Bruntwood Prize is that opportunity. It changed my life."

**Gareth Farr**
Judges Prize winner of The Bruntwood Prize for Playwriting 2011
for his play *Britannia Waves The Rules*

**Over our 40-year history as one of Manchester's largest property companies, Bruntwood has always played an active part in the city and its community.**

We are family owned and run, and have a strong belief that what is good for the cities we operate in is good for our customers and good for our business. That's why we are committed to pledging 10% of our annual profits to supporting the arts and other charitable and environmental activities.

# BIRD

Katherine Chandler

Thanks to:

The young people of Yellow, Bridgend.

Rachel O'Riordan, Suzanne Bell and Sarah Frankcom.

Georgia Henshaw, Siwan Morris, Guy Rhys, Connor Allen, Rosie Sheehy, Keiron Self, Lowri Palfrey, Claire Cage, Rehanna MacDonald, Oliver Morgan Thomas, Laura Elsworthy, Beatrice Scirocchi, Harry Attwell, Owen Whitelaw, Leah Walker.

Róisín McBrinn, Imogen Knight and the National Theatre Studio.

Guy O'Donnell, Mali O'Donnell and Mathonwy O'Donnell – always for you.

My Grampy, for whistling deaf aids and pipes that are dummies and donkey beach, and hard-boiled eggs that put hairs on your chest and sausage, beans and chips in Rabiotti's.

*K.C.*

*For my family*

## Characters

AVA, *fifteen*
TASH, *thirteen*
CLAIRE, *thirty-three*
DAN, *seventeen*
LEE, *forty*

*This text went to press before the end of rehearsals and so may differ slightly from the play as performed.*

AVA *and* TASH.

*A cliff.*

*A large stretch of water.*

AVA *stands at the tip of the cliff, the end of the earth, breathing it in.*

*Arms outstretched like wings.*

*Breathing.*

*Closes her eyes.*

*Breathes.*

*A rumble of noise begins.*

*Look up.*

*The sky.*

*Noise and movement through the sky.*

*Wonder.*

*Giggling behind her.*

*Noise and movement through the sky.*

*Giggling increases.*

TASH *grabs* AVA.

*The swell of noise increases.*

*Movements in the sky, shadows. Birds.*

*Fly over randomly.*

*Increasing in numbers.*

TASH *and* AVA *look at each other.*

*Hold each other's gaze.*

*TASH grabs AVA's hands.*

*They giggle.*

*Hold hands spinning together.*

*Looking at each other, laughing with each other.*

*Spinning together, they watch the birds with delight, still holding hands.*

*Birds.*

| | |
|---|---|
| AVA | What do you think they are? |
| | *Watches the sky.* |
| | *Watches.* |
| TASH | Free. |
| | *They let go of each other and fall to the floor.* |
| | CLAIRE *in a café.* |
| AVA | I sent you letters. |
| | I didn't have your number. |
| | *No response.* |
| | I would have texted. |
| | It felt weird. |
| | Posh like. |
| | Sending you letters. I put 'Dear Mam'. |
| | I thought if it was a text. |
| | I think I would have put, 'Alright' or something like that. |
| | But with letters. |
| | It's weird init. |
| | Did you get them? |
| | I never knew. |
| | So I just kept writing them. |
| | Like on them shows when they gets lost family together and stuff they says that don't they. |

They says 'For years I got you a birthday card'
and they shows them a big pile of cards and
Christmas presents and stuff.
When is your birthday?
I was thinking I don't know when your birthday is.
I know it's March some time but I don't know
exactly when.
Cos we could do something couldn't we. We could
do something nice.

Did you get the letters?

CLAIRE     I got them.

AVA        I didn't know.

CLAIRE     I can't read much, as it goes.

AVA        I didn't know that.
           I never knew that about you.

CLAIRE     Well, now you do.

AVA        I didn't think.
           It makes sense.
           Now I'm thinking of it, that makes sense of a lot
           of things.

CLAIRE     I'm glad.

AVA        Forms an' stuff.
           It makes sense.
           Anything official.
           I can help with that.

CLAIRE     I get by.

AVA        Paul likes his forms.
           Me and Tash. She's my friend.
           Me and Tash laughs about that.
           But he's alright is Paul. They're not all like him.
           Social workers. But he is.
           He'd help you. With your reading an' that. Forms.

CLAIRE     I get by.
           I said.

AVA         I thought you could come by, you know and or we
            can do this. Meet. And. Start. It's a start.

CLAIRE      You know what Ava means?
            Bird.
            That's what you are.
            You're a little bird.

AVA         I thought. I thought it would be.
            Get back to normal.

            Then in time,        CLAIRE      Flitting and
            you know.                         flying from one
                                              thing to another.

CLAIRE      Won't no one ever cage you in, Ava. You needs to
            be free.
            You're like me.

            *Plays with her handbag.*

            I haven't got much time so.

AVA         Got things to do have you?

CLAIRE      I have as it goes.

AVA         It's been three years.

CLAIRE      Has it.

AVA         It has, yes.

CLAIRE      So you're sixteen? Are you?

AVA         Fifteen.

CLAIRE      I thought.
            I knew it was fifteen.
            The numbers gets jumbled. The years.
            Fifteen.

AVA         I'm sixteen next month.

CLAIRE      I had you when I was sixteen.

            *Pause.*

We used to come here.
When you was little.
On a Friday.
You'd have sausage, beans and chips and we'd get two forks.
You could never eat a whole plate of food.
Pecking away at it.
And milkshake. You'd have milkshake.

AVA        Don't like it now.

CLAIRE     No.

*Long pause.*

CLAIRE *plays with her cigarette pack.*

AVA        I need to talk to you. I'll be sixteen and it all changes. You know.

CLAIRE *offers nothing. Plays with her phone.*

Will you give me your number?
I could text you.

CLAIRE *puts down her phone.*

You can have mine.
Send me a message on my birthday. Stuff like that.

CLAIRE     I don't know.

AVA        You don't know?

CLAIRE     They worry about contact you know. They have rules.
I don't know if I'm allowed.

AVA        It's a number.
That's all.

CLAIRE

AVA        I wouldn't phone, you know.
Just emergencies.

Then I'd know where you were.
You could text me.

*Stops.*

We could go for a walk?

| | |
|---|---|
| CLAIRE | Where? |
| AVA | Outside. |
| CLAIRE | Why? |
| AVA | I just thought. |
| CLAIRE | You just thought. |
| AVA | On the front. |
| CLAIRE | No. |
| AVA | On the beach. |
| CLAIRE | I'm fine where I am. |
| AVA | By the sea. |
| CLAIRE | It's cold. Too cold. And I hate the sand. |

This place.
Christ.
That fair.
How there's not been an accident.
It's not safe.
Should be condemned. When the train stopped
I thought.
It's like a ghost town here.
Doesn't look the same. It's, I dunno, neglected.

| | |
|---|---|
| AVA | You got the train? |
| CLAIRE | Yes. |
| AVA | Not driving then. |
| CLAIRE | No. |
| AVA | How long did it take? On the train? |

CLAIRE     About an hour, I think.

AVA        So you live about an hour away?

           *Nothing.*

           You moved.

CLAIRE

AVA        Where do you live?

CLAIRE     We wanted a fresh start.
           Somewhere nobody knew about us.
           About all the lies.

AVA        They weren't lies.

           *Pause.*

CLAIRE     What do you want, Ava?

           When your social worker called, he said you
           wanted to meet me and I thought, I thought to
           myself then, there'll be something. She's after
           something.

AVA        They can't support me where I am, Paul said.
           They would if they could. Fucking government.
           That's what Paul says. Privilege, he talks about
           that all the time and capitalism and Fucking
           Thatcher – he really hates her. That's where it all
           went wrong Paul says, with her.

           *Stops.*

           I've got choices to make.

CLAIRE     I didn't have to come.
           But I'm here.
           I'm under no obligation, that's what that Paul said.
           So I don't have to do nothing.
           It's not that I have to.
           I just thought. I would.
           We thought.
           I'm here.

AVA

I went there.
To the house.
About a year ago. I thought about it a lot. And
I thought I'll just go. There's nothing. Nobody to
stop me. What can they do. An' I'm thinking all
day what to wear cos I don't know why but
I wanted to look, it was important you know,
I wanted to look good.
An' on the train all the way there I'm thinking
about what I'm gonna say, how clever I'm gonna
talk. I think of all this stuff to talk about and then
I gets off the train and I can't remember a word of
it. It's all gone mashed up in me head. An' I'm
thinking about getting back on the train but I
forces myself to keep on walking and I gets there.
To the house and I sees a family through the
window and it ain't my family.
And I walks next door just to check and I knocks
the door and Lesley Jacks answers and she nearly
fell on the floor when she sees me like but she says
'She've gone. Been gone over a year.' She didn't
know where you was, didn't care to know neither.
So you moved.
I knew that.
You didn't know, I knew that.
I knew you moved.

CLAIRE

What d'you ask me for then?

AVA

Where do you live?
Where d'you live now?

CLAIRE

I cried when you went.
Do you know that?
I cried.
Looking at you with your things in a bag.

AVA

A bin bag.

CLAIRE

It was hard for me.

AVA

I remember that.

| | |
|---|---|
| CLAIRE | I really tried with you. |
| AVA | All my things in a bin bag. |
| CLAIRE | It's all about you. |
| AVA | Waiting for them to pick me up. |
| CLAIRE | Always about you. |
| AVA | You had a choice. |
| CLAIRE | I knew you'd be okay. |
| AVA | You don't know I'm okay.<br>Cos you didn't give a shit so long as you was.<br>You was okay. |
| CLAIRE | I was okay? Jesus. After what you did. |
| AVA | *I* did. Is that what you thinks? Is that what you still thinks? |
| CLAIRE | Calm down. |
| AVA | After what *he* did. |
| CLAIRE | People are looking. |
| AVA | What do you care? |
| CLAIRE | I care about you making a show of us. |
| AVA | Give me your number. Your mobile. |
| CLAIRE | Contact has to be arranged, you can't just give me a call, like that. |
| AVA | Your address? |
| CLAIRE | They won't be happy with that. |
| AVA | Don't do that. |
| CLAIRE | What? |
| AVA | Sit there fucking lying to me. Contact an' all that shit.<br>Them and they.<br>Just give me your fucking number or don't. |

Give me your fucking address or don't.
Don't fucking lie.

CLAIRE    Watch your mouth.

AVA    Why?

*Pause.*

CLAIRE *puts her phone in her bag.*

CLAIRE    Look. I'm here. I came. I thought something about
you might have changed.
But it don't seem like that's the case. I don't think
this is gonna work.
It's a mistake.

*Pause.*

I think I should go.

AVA    No.

*Pause.*

I'm sorry.

*Pause.*

Mum.
I want to come home.

CLAIRE *stands.*

TASH    When I was five.

AVA    Tash?

TASH    Did I tell you this?

AVA    Are you here, Tash?

CLAIRE *leaves the scene.*

TASH    Did I tell you about when I was five, Ava?

AVA    I can't see you.

TASH    Close your eyes.

AVA *closes her eyes and* TASH *is next to her.*
*Whispers in her ear.*

When I was five.

AVA *giggles, opens her eyes.*

AVA        When I was five.

TASH       Me dad taught me to swim.

AVA        I haven't got a dad.

TASH       In the Irish Sea.

AVA        I had me granddad.

TASH       If you can swim in the Irish Sea you can swim
           anywhere.
           Did you know that, Ava?

AVA        Me granddad was deaf. And he had this pipe. His
           dummy he'd call it. It was never out of his mouth.

TASH       And when I was six.

AVA        When I was six.

           TASH *giggles.*

TASH       I'm sure I told you this.

AVA        I had me granddad. His deaf aid whistled.

TASH       Me dad took me down the sea. The Irish Sea. And
           taught me how to hold me breath underwater. He
           timed me. I could hold me breath for ninety-three
           seconds. That's one minute and thirty-three
           seconds, that is. And that's above average.

AVA        We'd go to Donkey Beach.
           He'd take me crabbing.

TASH       Me dad said I should be grateful, be grateful for
           two healthy lungs. Grateful I could breathe. He
           was teaching me lessons cos me mam died.
           He was good like that me dad.

AVA    We'd have hard-boiled eggs me and me granddad
       and we'd peel the shells and there'd always be a
       crunch on them from the sand and he'd say – good
       for you that, put hairs on yer chest. And we'd laff.

TASH   Me nana said me mam died having me.

AVA    I think I'd have been alright if he didn't die.
       Me granddad.

TASH   She didn't though.
       Me nana lied.
       She lied all the time.
       Me mam died of asthma, me dad told me.
       Coughed herself to death.

AVA    She don't want me home, Tash. I could see it in her.

TASH   I want you.

AVA    Will I be homeless?

TASH   No.

AVA    Is that what happens? To us? Is that what this is?

TASH   No.

AVA    It happens.

TASH   Not to you. I won't let it.

       DAN *at the park*.

AVA    But it happens.

DAN    Why do you come here?

TASH   Not to you.

DAN    You're always here, I see you.

TASH   Do you hear me? Ava?

       *Movements in the sky, shadows.*

       *Birds.*

       Not to you.

| | |
|---|---|
| DAN | Why d'ya come here? |
| AVA | Dunno. |
| DAN | I never sees kids here.<br>Which is weird cos it's like a park an' all. |
| | TASH *leaves the scene.* |
| AVA | Would you bring your kids here? |
| | DAN *looks around.* |
| DAN | Will you leave school d'you think? |
| AVA | Yeah. |
| DAN | In July. |
| AVA | June. |
| DAN | What will you do? |
| AVA | Don't know. |
| DAN | Work? |
| AVA | Maybe. |
| DAN | College? |
| AVA | No. |
| DAN | You could.<br>You could go to the tech. |
| AVA | I won't. |
| DAN | I seen you the other day down the coast. |
| AVA | I goes down there sometimes. |
| DAN | You was with someone. |
| AVA | Something to do. |
| DAN | Some old guy. |
| AVA | I like the coast. |
| DAN | He's there all the time. |

| | |
|---|---|
| AVA | I like the sea. |
| DAN | I like your mouth. |
| AVA | What? |
| DAN | Sorry. |
| AVA | What was you doing down the coast? |
| DAN | I was there with me dad and me brother. He takes us there, me dad. To fish. |
| AVA | In that sea. It's brown. It's like brown runny shit. I wouldn't eat nothing from there. |
| DAN | We don't.<br>He says he does.<br>He kills them with a stick.<br>He's the last one. Fishing like that. He's done it all his life. His old man taught him. At the estuary. When the tide goes out he walks the coast. He knows all the dips and troughs. He's got a stick, like a harpoon thing, it's like a fork with three blades. Looks like Nemo. |
| AVA | He looks like a fish? |
| DAN | King Nemo, the one with the beard.<br>And the fork thing. |
| | AVA *giggles*. |
| AVA | Neptune. You mean Neptune. |
| DAN | He stands calm as you like and waits. And then he stabs down into the water and the fish comes out flapping and jumping on the end of his fork. Then he takes it home and guts it. |
| AVA | He eats it? |
| DAN | He freezes them. He says he's going to eat them later but he never does. He feels guilty. I've sometimes seen him cry when they die. |
| AVA | Why does he do it? |

DAN    Because of his dad.

AVA    Can you do it?

DAN    He takes us there but I only goes cos I know I gets
       chips after.

AVA    I hoped you could do it.

DAN    What?

AVA    I hoped you could fish.
       It would have been something about you that was
       interesting.

DAN    Nothing interesting about me. Sorry.

AVA    Do you live at home?

DAN    Yeah.

AVA    You've got a brother.

DAN    And a sister.
       She's younger.

AVA    You live at home.
       With your family.

       Why are you here?

DAN    What?

AVA    Why did you come here?

DAN    I just did.

AVA    To see me.

DAN    No.

AVA    But you knew I'd be here.

       *Nothing.*

DAN    Sorry.

AVA    He's not old.
       The man at the coast.

| | |
|---|---|
| DAN | He drives a taxi. |
| AVA | You like my mouth. |
| DAN | Yeah, I do yeah. |
| | It's. You know.<br>I like it.<br>I like looking at it. |
| AVA | Don't. |
| DAN | What? |
| AVA | Like it. |
| DAN | Don't like your mouth? |
| AVA | Yes. |
| DAN | Okay.<br>I just, you know.<br>I was just saying.<br>Trying to say something nice. |
| AVA | Well don't.<br>It won't make any difference. |
| DAN | Any difference? |
| AVA | It won't work. |
| DAN | Work? |
| AVA | If I want to fuck you, I will.<br>What you say.<br>I like your hair.<br>Your eyes are the colour of… |
| DAN | I said I like your mouth. I dunno, I just.<br>It came into my head and said it.<br>I like your mouth. |
| AVA | Mouth, hair, eyes whatever.<br>It won't make the difference.<br>If I want to.<br>I will. |

DAN     Do you?

AVA     What?

DAN     Do you want to, you know?

        *No response.*

        *Tries another tactic.*

        Should we. D'you want to go out or something.
        We could go out.
        Some time.
        Not like just meet up here or the bus stop or
        properly go to a film or.

AVA     I like the bus stop.

DAN     Do you?

AVA     I like buses.
        I like to sit on buses because you're higher up than
        in a car.

DAN     I never thought of that.

        You didn't answer.

AVA     What?

DAN     Before.

AVA     Oh.

DAN     I asked you if you wanted to, you know?

AVA     No.

DAN     You're a prick-tease.

AVA     Am I.

DAN     I should.
        I could.

AVA     What?

DAN     Do you anyway.

*He grabs her.*

*Kisses her frenetically.*

*Pulls at her, puts his hand in her bra.*

*Tugs at his own clothes.*

AVA *doesn't react – totally apathetic.*

DAN *stops.*

I could.

AVA     You won't.

        I'm being honest.

DAN     I don't know why you're here.

AVA     Life is easier that way, I think.

DAN     Why do you come here?

AVA     I'm making friends.

DAN     You want me to be honest?

AVA     Yes.

        *Tries to kiss her.*

        Don't.

DAN     I thought you said.

        I just want to kiss you.
        Like friends.
        In a friendly way.

AVA     Be honest.

DAN     I'm being honest.

        *A silence,* DAN *considers his next tactic.*
        AVA *knows it's coming.*

        Okay, you want me to be honest.

AVA     I do.

DAN I want to kiss you.
    But more than that I want to, you know.
    I'm not that interested in you or anything, just
    talking because that way you might say yes.
    That's what everyone says. They say to come here.
    You're known.
    They talk about you.
    Around here.
    Told me you'd be here. So, you know.
    And I thought. Why not. I'll give it a try.
    I don't care, you know, if you don't want to go out
    with me or whatever. And I don't give a shit about
    seeing a film with you or why you like the bus.
    I do like your mouth.
    I like your mouth because I think about putting
    my, you know, my… I think about my thing in it.
    That's why I'm here. I'm here because I'm all
    about that, it's like that when you're seventeen.
    My life is ruled by my dick.
    I'm hoping that fades but I'm not betting on it.

AVA You want to touch me.

DAN Yes.

AVA Tell me.

DAN I want to touch you.

AVA What do you want me to do?

DAN What?

AVA Tell me what you want and I'll do it.

DAN I want you to suck my dick.

    AVA *and* DAN *eye each other, raw.*

    LEE *at the coast.*

    *A taxi.*

    AVA *drops to her knees and undoes* DAN*'s*
    *trousers.*

LEE *plays Curtis Mayfield's 'Move On Up'.*

*Focus shifts to* LEE *as* AVA *stands and dances her way over to him, leaving* DAN.

DAN *zips himself up and leaves the scene.*

AVA *takes a can off* LEE *and opens it, swaying/dancing. Can in hand.*

AVA         'Losing My Religion'.
            That's a song I'd like to hear. Paul likes it, that
            song. Says it reminds him of being a student.
            Says he was a mental case. 'Mad for it' he says
            it like that.
            (*Shouts to the wind.*) 'Mad for it.'
            He's a total knob but I likes him.
            'Losing My Religion'. Have you got that. That
            song, Lee?

LEE         I haven't.

AVA         You know what I'm gonna do, Lee. I'm gonna get
            off my head.

LEE         Are you?

AVA         Have you got more?

            *Drains the can.*

            Lee. Leeee. Lee. It's a weird name that. What does
            it mean, Lee?

LEE         I don't know.

AVA         It's like it's not finished. Like it should be Liam or
            Leonardo. Lianne. Is it a mistake? It's a mistake,
            Lee. Are you a mistake?

            *Laughs.*

LEE         You know what are wankers?

AVA         Have you got any more?

LEE         Seagulls.
            Seagulls are wankers. Scavengers. They rips open

your bin bags. Do anything for food. You
remember that.

AVA    Should I look in the cab?

*Hands her a can.*

LEE    Birds of prey have got the reputation but it's the
gulls you needs to watch. I saw gulls capsize a
fishing boat once. Near enough took a man's arm
off just to get to the fish.
There was a story on the radio just last week about
posties being attacked by gulls who was nesting.
You know what they did? They put female posties
on the job.
Gulls didn't bother with them.
Left them to it.
Makes you think don't it.

AVA    My name means bird. Maybe I'm a gull, Lee.
It's German. I think it's German.
Tash is a Russian name.
From Anastasia.
I like that. I wish I had a Russian name.
They think she's still alive don't they, Anastasia,
from when they killed the Royals.
Me and Tash watched the film. Everyone thinks
she got away, Anastasia.
Tash thought she was still alive.
I think people tells themselves that cos it's shit
what they done. People do that don't they, lies to
themselves when things are bad.
I think they killed her.

They reckon they killed them with bayonets. The
princesses, bayonets in the head. That wasn't in
the film.
Not the Disney one.
She's dead.
She's definitely dead.

*AVA swaying/dancing/breathing in the air.*

| | |
|---|---|
| LEE | D'you know why I like it here? |
| AVA | You like the sea. |
| LEE | I like the sea. |
| AVA | Yes, you do. |
| LEE | I like it because of its noise. There's a rhythm to it. |
| AVA | I got rhythm, Lee.<br>I don't know where I gets it from. |
| LEE | I used to live by the sea. Up the coast. |
| AVA | I bet my mam's a shit dancer. |
| | *Laughs.* |
| LEE | Used to live in a B&B off the dock. |
| AVA | Maybe my dad, maybe my dad was a banging dancer, Lee, whoever he was. |
| LEE | Used to know when they was nesting off the dock. The noise. Jesus. The screaming and screeching. That'd last a couple of months all told. They nest on roofs an' all now. That's what they was doing with them posties. They was on the roofs of the houses. Swooping down at them.<br>Wankers. |
| | AVA *stops dancing. Swigs her can.* |
| AVA | Are you alright, Lee? |
| LEE | I am. Are you alright? |
| AVA | Yeah, I'm alright. |
| LEE | I'm glad you're here. |
| AVA | Got nowhere else, have I? |
| LEE | I wasn't sure you'd come. |
| AVA | But I did. |
| LEE | You did. |

AVA       Is it just cans you got, Lee? Have you got vodka?
          Like that one Tash was drinking?

LEE       Last summer I come here and there was a tree
          trunk washed up on the beach.
          I couldn't believe my eyes, Ava.
          Forty-foot long it was and covered in barnacles,
          all writhing and moving. Looked like some sort of
          sea monster. But it weren't of course.
          They reckons it come from America. Washed over
          from some hurricane they had.

AVA       Don't know what barnacles are?

LEE       We gets barnacle geese migrating here.
          Rare they are.
          A rare species.
          They swarms on the cliff there. Should see them,
          Ava, when they swarms.
          You'll never see a sight like it in your life.

          *AVA swigs more.*

          Nobody knows where they comes from. They
          don't have nests, see.
          They just appears.

          *LEE watches AVA.*

          When I first saw you and Tash. I thought of them.
          I thought of the barnacle geese.

AVA       I'd like to see them.
          Flying like that.
          I'd love to see them geese, Lee.

LEE       Remember, Ava, that first time. Right here. The
          wind nearly blew you both away and you was
          grabbing on to each other, young and free,
          laughing together, screaming wasn't you, with the
          wind, dancing together, with the wind blowing
          through you both.

AVA       I remember.

| | |
|---|---|
| LEE | And then the rain. Big sheets of it. Bouncing off the coast. |
| AVA | And we ran to you and got in the cab. We didn't have no money. |
| LEE | Hitting the sea it was. So furious you wouldn't know where the sea starts and the rain ends. |
| AVA | We sat in the cab and had a right laugh, didn't we, Lee. |
| LEE | I likes the sea, Ava.<br>The sea never changes.<br>We could have been sat here twenty year ago and if we looked out to sea it would have been the same. Hundred year ago. The same.<br>Thousand years even.<br>But if you turns around and looks at them houses there.<br>Twenty year ago. They had windows, not boarded up like that.<br>The paint weren't off and peeled like it is now.<br>Hundred year ago them houses would've been standing there all proud.<br>Rich people would've lived there. People who worked the docks. Shipping merchants. Proud, wealthy people.<br>It'll come round.<br>Someone's gonna see the value of the land here and they'll demolish them houses.<br>They'll build flats or whatever for money.<br>Twenty years from now we'd be looking at flats.<br>It'll all change.<br>I don't like change, Ava. I like to be certain of things.<br>The sea.<br>It'll be the same. |

LEE *hands* AVA *a bottle of vodka.*

You can't buy the sea.
Not much in life that don't have a price.

LEE *picks up a new iPhone.*

I like to be reminded of that.

AVA *drinks from the bottle.*

I got you this.

*He hands* AVA *the iPhone.*

AVA *squeals with delight.*

AVA     They cost a fucking fortune.

LEE     Not gonna cost you a penny. Not a thing.
        That's yours.

AVA     Thank you, Lee.

LEE     I'll call you on that, I put my number in, so
        you'll know it's me. And you're in mine so
        I'll know it's you.

        AVA *is playing with the phone, not paying
        attention to* LEE.

        LEE *fiddles with the radio.*

AVA     Tonight, I'm gonna get off my fucking head.

        LEE *finds the song and REM's 'Losing My
        Religion' starts to play.*

        AVA *squeals and hugs* LEE.

        *Jumps up, swigging her can and losing herself
        in the song.*

        *From REM to the cliff.*

        AVA*'s drunk lost dancing.*

        *Alone.*

        *Closes her eyes.*

*More formal dancing.*

*Northern Soul.*

*Smiles to herself.*

TASH *is dancing away from* AVA.

*Not in time, not together.*

*Slowly their pacing becomes timed. They dance the same steps. Still apart. In time they come together.*

TASH *comes to* AVA.

*Having fun with it.*

*Dancing and laughing.*

| | |
|---|---|
| TASH | Know what that is? |
| AVA | No. |
| TASH | That's Northern Soul that is. |
| | It's the best dancing there is. Me dad said it's dancing from the soul. Can you feel it, Ava? |
| AVA | I can feel it. |
| TASH | Me dad taught me to dance. On me seventh birthday he took me here. Right here, Ava, to the edge of the world and he taught me. And he said forget about them discos and clubs and parties. He said this is where you dance, Ava, right here at the edge of the world with the wind in your hair and the salt water on your skin. You'll feel the pound of the earth he said and there ain't a beat like it. |

*They stand together and breathe in the air.*

There are other worlds, Ava. Other places than this.

AVA *giggles.*

What you laughing at, you?

| | |
|---|---|
| AVA | I don't know about that. |

TASH     I do.

AVA

TASH     He had a thing, my dad, a thing about the stars and
         all that. Parallel universes and parallel lives. He
         always said, he said this a lot, that if this world
         weren't working for you then just close your eyes
         and think of a world that is. Cos chances are, things
         are fine for you somewhere else, in another world.

         He said in another life he would have been a star
         doctor.
         For a job.
         They have them. They do, Ava. A doctor for
         the stars.
         Can you imagine if your dad was a star doctor.
         But in this world that wasn't him. Me dad.
         Not in this life, he said.

AVA      When you was eight.

TASH     When I was eight.

AVA      He went when you was eight.

TASH     He broke my heart.

AVA      Broke your heart in two.

TASH     It's when it all changed.

AVA      Your dad said, it wasn't right that his girl had
         never seen a night sky as it should be seen.

TASH     That's what he said.

AVA      He told your nana.

TASH     And he was getting all worked up.

AVA      And he says 'We're off.' He says 'I'm taking my
         girl to Exmoor.'

TASH     And she sits there, smoking a fag, taking it all in.
         He says, 'My girl,' like this he says it, 'My girl will

see a night sky that would live with her for ever.'
He says 'She'll see three thousand stars
shimmering and twinkling in a sky the colour
of ink.
She'll see shooting stars…

AVA        …And the Milky Way.'

TASH       Then he grabs a carrier bag and he shoves some
           things in it and he grabs me arm and he says to
           her, he says 'I'm going,' he says, 'I'm taking my
           girl to Exmoor, just you see.'

AVA        And she just sits there.

TASH       'That's it I'm off,' he says. 'There's another life,
           another life for us and I'm gonna take her there.'
           And he's still got my arm and this bag and she
           looks at me and opens her bag and gives him a
           note. Twenty I thinks.

AVA        And he near enough pulls your arm off.

TASH       And we goes down the stairs and out, down
           Coronation Terrace and we turns the corner and
           then I realises he's not there.
           I'm on me own.
           And I stands there for a while. Waiting.
           And waiting.

AVA        He don't come back.

TASH       After a while I goes back to the house.
           And in me head I tells myself he's magic.
           I tells myself he's gone to the other world he
           always talks about.
           It's what he done.
           The drugs made him behave that way.
           We can't help it, Ava.
           The things we do.
           People.

AVA/TASH   We do what we do.

We can't escape from what we are.
Even when we hates ourselves for it.

*Shadows and birds.*

LEE *watches the shadows.*

AVA *leaves* TASH.

TASH *dancing on her own.*

CLAIRE *searches in her bag. Pulls out a picture.
Slaps it in front of* AVA.

AVA *looks at the image.*

*Takes a while to ingest it.*

*Looks to* CLAIRE.

AVA         Who's that?
            Who is it?

CLAIRE      She's why I'm here.

            *Looks at the photo.*

AVA         Is it me?

            *Grabs at* CLAIRE.

            Is that me, is it?
            Is it me?

CLAIRE      I had a baby, Ava.

AVA         I don't get it. I can't.

CLAIRE      Not such a baby now, mind.

AVA         I don't understand.

CLAIRE      I was pregnant when you left.

            *Pause.*

AVA         She? You said she?

CLAIRE      You needed to know.

| | |
|---|---|
| AVA | I've got a sister? |
| CLAIRE | And now you do. |
| AVA | I never thought. |
| CLAIRE | I want all our cards on the table. |
| AVA | I didn't even think that. A baby.<br>You weren't pregnant. |
| CLAIRE | I was. Five months. |
| AVA | Does she know about me? |
| CLAIRE | She don't know. |
| AVA | You haven't told her about me? |
| CLAIRE | I been talking to     AVA     I'm her sister.<br>that Paul. |
| AVA | Paul? |
| CLAIRE | Talking things through. |

AVA *taking it all in*.

| | |
|---|---|
| AVA | I got a sister. |
| CLAIRE | I didn't have any brothers or sisters.<br>It was just me and your granddad. |
| AVA | How old is she? |
| CLAIRE | I didn't phone about that. Not about her. I wanted<br>to talk it over. What you said. About coming<br>home. |

*Still trying to take it all in*.

| | |
|---|---|
| AVA | When I left? You said. So she's three or two.<br>Is she two? |
| CLAIRE | I never thought about you coming back. |
| | I don't know why you would think of it. |
| AVA | She's two. |

CLAIRE      Paul said it was common.

            *Pause.*

            He didn't think it was a good idea.

AVA         Paul wouldn't say that.

CLAIRE      I don't have to.
            You'll be sixteen.
            So.

AVA         What's her name?

CLAIRE      Said you was still dealing with your anger.

AVA         Does she look like me?

CLAIRE      I told him best of luck with that. You always had
            a temper. Always difficult.

AVA         A sister.

CLAIRE      Always pushed it too far.

            AVA *puts down the photo.*

AVA         I want to see her.

            CLAIRE *shuffles in her seat.*

CLAIRE      There's places you can go.
            Accommodation.
            It's not like you're thrown out on the street.

            *Pause.*

AVA         She'll want me home. You know, to be... I can be
            her sister.

CLAIRE      It's not your home.

            *Pause.*

AVA         I can help you with her.

CLAIRE      You what?

AVA         She can get to know me.

CLAIRE     No.

AVA        I can. I thought, I can help you.

CLAIRE     I can't have you in the house.

           AVA *taking it in*.

AVA        But you told me. You told me about her.

CLAIRE     I won't have you in the house. With her. Jesus.

           *Time*.

AVA        Why did you tell me about her?

CLAIRE     So you'd know.

AVA        I won't be no bother. I swear.

CLAIRE     Why would you ask? Why would you even think
           of it? We haven't seen you in three years.

AVA        I won't say nothing to her. About what happened.
           I swear she won't know nothing, not from me. She
           don't need to know none of that about him.

CLAIRE     What are you talking about?

AVA        I won't tell her.

CLAIRE     You can't help yourself.

AVA        I need to come home.

CLAIRE     We're a family. Happy.

           *Pause*.

           *Three seconds*.

AVA        I'll change. I've changed. I'll be good, I swear.
           Please.

CLAIRE     You won't.
           You can't.
           You was born fighting and raging.
           You screamed for the first six months. Day and
           night. I don't know how I'd have coped if it
           weren't for my dad.

You never wanted me.
Men.
You always took to men.

I don't want you home.

AVA *is still. Takes it in.*

*Three seconds.*

AVA         Was this his idea?

CLAIRE      I'm not talking to you about him.

AVA         Coming here? Doing this to me? Is this him?

CLAIRE      He wanted to forgive you.

AVA         This is him.

CLAIRE      What you put him through and he wanted to
            forgive you.
            He was willing for you to come back.

AVA

CLAIRE      But I don't want you there.
            Cos I know what you're like.
            You was all over him then.
            Wouldn't leave him alone.
            He was embarrassed by you.

AVA         I wasn't.

CLAIRE      You wanted everything I had.

AVA         I didn't, I never did.

CLAIRE      You took everything from me.

            Does that make it easier does it? To think it's him.

AVA         I'm thinking about it here. I'm thinking it about
            it all what you just done and it feels like it's him,
            is all.

CLAIRE      I can think for myself.

AVA         I know him.

CLAIRE     You don't know him.

AVA        But I do though.

CLAIRE     He's my husband.

AVA        I know him and it seems to me. It feels like to me
           that he's here. Telling you what to do and you
           don't even know it.

CLAIRE     Tell me about him.

AVA        What?

CLAIRE     If you knows him so well then tell me.

AVA        I told you about him but you don't listen.

CLAIRE     His dad was an alcoholic.
           Didn't know that, did you.

           No?

           He was nine when he found out who his dad were.
           Or that, didn't know that did you. Mrs 'I Know
           Him So Well'.

           *Nothing.*

           Nine and one day he comes home from school and
           his mam's sat in the kitchen and she's crying –
           'Lad, you know you wants to know about your
           father, well his name's Jonno and he's sat in the
           front room.'
           – And he was.
           You didn't know that.
           He never told you about that stuff, did he?
           About how Jonno made their lives hell. A living
           hell.
           You think you knows all about him but you don't
           know nothing.
           The person he fucked knows that stuff.
           Me.
           I. Knows. him.

AVA        Let me come home.

           *Time*.

           I didn't tell them. I didn't tell the social nothing.

CLAIRE     You had nothing to tell them.
           They would have charged him if you had.
           We couldn't cope. You were destroying us.

AVA        He wasn't charged. They didn't charge him
           because I didn't say nothing.

CLAIRE     What?

AVA        They couldn't.
           Because of me.

CLAIRE     Are you some sort of fantasist. Is that what you
           are? Sat there bare-faced.

AVA        I wasn't. I didn't disclose.

CLAIRE     We called the social services. We did.

AVA        You left me with him.

CLAIRE     We called them because of you.
           Not because of him.

AVA        When Granddad died. You left me with him.

CLAIRE     My dad.

AVA        You weren't there.

CLAIRE     My dad had died. I was heartbroken. And I came
           back to you and your lies.

AVA        I only told you.

CLAIRE     We called the social services.
           Because of you.
           Not because of him.

           I couldn't cope with you.

AVA          I'm fifteen. Sixteen nearly.
             A woman. A fully grown woman.
             I'm no good to him now.

CLAIRE       What is in your head?
             What is in your fucking head.
             He don't.
             He's not interested in you.

             He was never interested in you.
             You was there walking around the place with next
             to nothing on and he wanted me. And you couldn't
             handle it.
             He wanted Me.
             Always did.
             He was fucking me.
             All that time.
             Why would he want you?
             He fucked me.
             Not you.
             Me.

             CLAIRE *picks up her bag to leave.*

             I can't do this no more.

             *Takes the photo off* AVA.
             AVA *grabs for it.*

             AVA *grabs at* CLAIRE.

AVA          Please. Don't. I won't say nothing. I won't.
             I won't say a word again.

             Please.

             *Movements in the sky, shadows.*

             *Birds.*

             TASH *makes shadow birds.*

             AVA *dances through them past* TASH.

             *Shadow birds.*

             AVA *dances the moves she learnt with* TASH.

LEE        You didn't come.

           AVA *carries on dancing*.

AVA        No.

LEE        I was here.

AVA        I been going down the park.

LEE        I was here.

AVA        And I was in the park.

LEE        A week since I saw you last.
           Got me to thinking.
           First I was worried, thinking all sorts of things
           after what happened.

AVA        I'm here.

LEE        I called you.

AVA        It's on silent.

LEE        Is it.

AVA        I thought you didn't want no one knowing about
           the phone?

LEE        It's just for you and me.

AVA        Well then.

LEE        I thought you and me understood each other.
           Thought we was sticking together.
           Looking out for each other.
           You and me.

           AVA *dances*.

           *Flirty. Tries to engage* LEE. *Provocative*.

           Stop it.

           I said stop.

           Cut it out.

AVA         Tash taught me. On her birthday last year we done
            a dance. She had a party. Paul done her a party cos
            she was thirteen, a teenager, and we done this
            dance. We had a right laugh.

            AVA *teases him, dancing closer.*

LEE         (*Sharp.*) I said cut it out.

            *A long pause.*

            You're worth more than that.

            AVA *leans into the taxi and turns the music up.*

            *Too loud.*

            *Dances.*

            Jesus.

            LEE *takes it for so long then turns it off.*

AVA         Hey.

LEE         Anything wrong with that.
            With this.
            It's called peace.

AVA         Listen to yourself.

LEE         Called being able to hear yourself think.

AVA         You're so old. Sounds like an old man.

LEE         The whole worlds. Noise. Buzzing and beeping
            and ringing.
            Full of noise. It does my nut in.
            There are times when it does my nut in, Ava.

AVA         Put it back on, Lee. I wanna dance.

LEE         I don't want you down the park.

AVA         What?

LEE         You're not to go there.

AVA         To the park?

| | |
|---|---|
| LEE | I thought something happened. And then I phoned and you don't answer. And I got you that phone didn't I.<br>Where does that leave me?<br>It's not what I thought this was. |
| AVA | I was just hanging out. |
| LEE | I thought about you, that's all. |
| AVA | I'm sorry. |
| LEE | I'm having a bad time with it all, as it goes. |
| AVA | Was you worried about me? |
| LEE | I look out for you, don't I?<br>After what happened.<br>I thought there was an understanding.<br><br>I don't want you to feel bad. |
| AVA | I don't. |
| LEE | You have no obligation to come here. |
| AVA | I know. |
| LEE | You don't owe me. Even after all I've done for you. But I thought.<br>Forget it. You're here. |
| AVA | I am.<br>Did you miss me? |
| LEE | You said, 'See you tomorrow.' |
| AVA | What? |
| LEE | Last time. 'See you tomorrow.'<br>A week ago. |
| AVA | Did I? |
| LEE | You did. |
| AVA | Can we put the music back on, Lee? |
| LEE | See you tomorrow. |

| AVA | But it don't mean that.<br>It's like, 'laters' or see you around or you know. |
|-----|-----|
| LEE | So that was a lie. |
| AVA | Not a lie. Just. |
| LEE | You lied to me. |
| AVA | No. It's just what you say. |
| LEE | 'See you tomorrow.' |
| AVA | Yeah. |
| LEE | You lied to me. |
| AVA | Put it back on, Lee. You can dance with me.<br>We can have a laugh. |
| LEE | Don't feel much like laughing. |

*AVA, suggestive again.*

*He looks at her.*

*Watches her dancing suggestively.*

*She moves over to him.*

*Closer.*

*Closer.*

*Moves her hand over him.*

*Puts it on his crotch.*

*After some time he looks her in the eye.*

Don't do that.

It's cheap.

*He turns away.*

| AVA | Did I do something wrong, Lee? |
|-----|-----|
| LEE | No. |
| AVA | I'm sorry. |

LEE        What you sorry for?

AVA        For not coming.

           *Pause.*

           My mam.
           She don't want me there. So.

LEE        You got nowhere to go.

AVA        I don't know what I'll do.

           Sorry I didn't come, Lee.

LEE        It's forgotten.

           AVA *moves to him.*

           *She touches his face.*

           *He lets her.*

           *She giggles.*

           LEE *grabs her hand.*

           AVA *says nothing.*

           I phoned you. And you didn't answer.

AVA

LEE        You always got your phone, you. Haven't you?

AVA        Not always.

           *Pause.*

LEE        Technology. You lot and your technology. Constant
           noise. The noise does my nut in. Buzzing and
           bleeping. Shall I tell you about technology, Ava.

AVA        If you like.

LEE        Don't get me wrong I uses it as much as the next
           fella. That's what you're thinking ain't it. I uses it
           all the fucking time.

You do an' all, Ava. That's why I got you that.
Armour. That's what it is. Like a shield around
ourselves.
We uses our phones so we don't have to talk to no
one. I sees it all the time. They gets in the cab and
starts on their phones so they don't have to talk to
me. That's okay. Suits me. I does it too. Just
something I noticed that's all. They texts people so
they don't have to speak. Emails an' all that shit.
All this stuff made for communication and the
irony is there ain't nobody communicating with no
one any more.
Not face to face, eye to eye.
They puts babies on their mothers immediately
when they're born.
Did you know that?

AVA    No.

LEE    Naked. Skin-to-skin they calls it. It's important.
That's how important it is.
Human contact.
Humankind.
Tash gave me that.
Like a gift.
And you. Looking at me face to face, eye to eye.
Without thought. Without judgement.
It's a quality you have.
A beautiful unadulterated.
Your innocence.

AVA    I'm not innocent, Lee.

*He looks at her.*

*A long time.*

What's wrong?

LEE    Nothing.
Look at you.

AVA    Then what's going on, Lee?

LEE         I can't do that.

            *Pause.*

            It's not that I can't.

AVA         I didn't think that.

LEE         There's nothing wrong with me or nothing.

            I don't do animals or shit like that.

            It's you been coming here, haven't you.
            You been coming to me.
            You and Tash come to me.
            That's all I'm saying.
            You understand.

AVA         I think so.

LEE         It's been you.
            Coming here.

AVA         I s'pose.

LEE         It has though.

AVA         Okay.

            *Thinks.*

            But you wants me here?

LEE         If that's what you want.

AVA         Buying me things. You buy me things. Give me
            things.

LEE         You didn't come, not for a week.
            But forget that.

AVA         You should have said.
            You wants me here.
            You should have told me.

LEE         I have things in the cab. Lager. CDs.
            They're there. Money.
            For you.

You can have whatever you wants.
You knows that.
I know it's been tough.
I'm the only one you got who knows how tough
it's been.

Your choice though. At the end of the day.

AVA     You was pissed off when I didn't come.

LEE     Not pissed off.

AVA     You was.

LEE     A bit but. Forget it.
Let's forget it.
You're here now.

AVA     You can't do what?

LEE     What?

AVA     You said 'I can't do that.'
What can't you do?

LEE     I don't want you talking like that.

AVA     Women?
You can't do Women? Sex?

LEE     There has been.
Girls.
I've had women.

I'm not a, I'm not weird am I.
I think you know that about me.

AVA     I do.

LEE     I'm not weird or some sort of pervert.

AVA     No.

LEE     You know that about me.

AVA     Yes.

LEE     You know me.

| | |
|---|---|
| AVA | I think so. |
| LEE | I have things in my head. |
| AVA | What things? |
| LEE | And I thought. |

Things take you by surprise.
Tash.
And you took me by surprise.
Here.

LEE *hands her a bottle of vodka.*

Drink it.

AVA *gulps it down.*

Will you stop coming?

| | |
|---|---|
| AVA | No. |
| LEE | Drink up. |

AVA *drinks.*

Can I trust you, Ava?

| | |
|---|---|
| AVA | Yes. |
| LEE | Can I? |
| AVA | Yes. |
| LEE | Are we there? |

At that place of trust.
Is that where we are?

| | |
|---|---|
| AVA | I think so. |
| LEE | Because this is us, Ava. |

If this is us.
If this is that, then there's no going back.

Do you understand, Ava?

| | |
|---|---|
| AVA | I think so. |
| LEE | Why aren't you drinking? |

AVA         I don't want any more.

LEE         Drink it.

            LEE *holds the bottle to her mouth and forces her*
            *to drink.*

AVA         I don't want any more, Lee.

            LEE *gets a knife from out of his pocket and slowly*
            *slices it into his palm making it bleed.*

            Lee. Your hand, Lee.

LEE         If you don't come it feels like this.
            That is what it feels like.
            Do you understand?
            Do you understand me, Ava?

            AVA *is shocked.*

AVA         Yes.

            *They look at each other.*

            Yes, I understand.

            LEE *takes the bottle and drinks from it himself.*

            *Leans back in the cab and puts the music back on.*

LEE         Come on.
            You wanted to dance, didn't you.

            AVA *says nothing.*

            Dance then.

            AVA *reluctantly dances, shaken.*

            LEE *watches.*

            *Joins her.*

            TASH *hiding.*

            AVA *dances.*

            *Away from* LEE.

TASH        Can you hear me, Ava?

|      | LEE *watches* AVA *for a bit*. |
|------|--------------------------------|
| AVA  | Are you here? |
| TASH | I'm here. |
|      | *A bird swoops past.* |
|      | *Catches* AVA*'s eye.* |
|      | Can you see me? |
|      | *Shadows, birds.* |
| AVA  | I can see you. |
|      | TASH *makes shadow puppets.* |
| TASH | I'll teach you to fly. |
| AVA  | You're mad, you. |
| TASH | If it gets too much, Ava<br>If it all gets too much. |
|      | We'll fly. |
|      | AVA *is stood on the edge of the cliff.* |
|      | TASH *is heard but not seen.* |
|      | Two little dickie birds<br>Sitting on a wall... |
|      | AVA *looks out to sea.* |
| AVA  | Fly away will we. |
|      | *A bird flies over.* |
|      | DAN *watches the shadows.* |
|      | AVA *looks around.* |
|      | What do you want? |
|      | TASH *has gone.* |
| DAN  | Nothing. I'm not here for anything. |
| AVA  | Right. |
| DAN  | I live round here. |

| | |
|---|---|
| AVA | You live round here? |
| DAN | Down Victoria Crescent. |
| AVA | The ones with the washing lines across the street? |
| DAN | So. It's not far. And I was just you know, passing. |
| AVA | I always liked that about them.<br>Do you have to share them? |
| DAN | What? |
| AVA | The washing lines? |
| DAN | No.<br>They... there's a system. You have the washing line to the left. |
| AVA | Like a pulley system. Linked to the house across the street.<br>I thought.<br>Once, I thought that Tash could live one side and me I'd live the other and we'd send messages over to each other.<br>Or a sister.<br>That's where I'd want to live.<br><br>I didn't know you lived there.<br>Them houses are small. That's why I liked them.<br>Cosy you know.<br>Is it small? |
| DAN | I shares with my brother. But my dad put a window in the attic and floorboards so. You know. |
| AVA | That's good. |
| DAN | Yeah. That is good. Cos now I can get away from my sister cos she's a fucking mentalist.<br>One minute laughing the next minute sobbing, everything's amazing or sick or horrendous.<br>My dad says it's her hormones but you know, |

whatever. I just wants out of it. So.
The attic is good.

Are you still in that place?

AVA     This is a shit park.

DAN     Why do you come here?

AVA     Something to do.

DAN     There's things to do.

AVA     I've got no money to do stuff, and stuff costs
money.

DAN     Do you still live in that place?

AVA     I have to leave. When I'm sixteen.

DAN     Move out?

AVA     Yep.

DAN     Shit.

AVA     It was mine and Tash's room.
We been there together since I, you know, since
I left. But.
I can't stay there after I'm sixteen.

DAN     Oh.

AVA     I don't want to.

DAN     No.

Where will you go?

AVA     Oh you know, Spain or somewhere exotic like that.

DAN     No shit?

AVA     Do I look like I'm going to Spain, Dan.

I wanted to go back with my mam, you know.
Back there. But.
That's not going to happen.
Paul's trying to help find me somewhere.
He will an' all. I don't want it to be far.

| | |
|---|---|
| DAN | I didn't think you had a home, you know, or family, or… I didn't think. That's a lie.<br>I did think but I was trying to, you know, to be polite.<br>Which is stupid I think because really I wanted to ask.<br>I didn't think you had a family. |
| AVA | I have.<br><br>I've got a sister. So I want to be there. For her. |
| DAN | That's good then. |
| AVA | I didn't know about her.<br>And now I do. So.<br>She's three.<br>I think she's about two or three. |
| DAN | Will you move away? |
| AVA | It's about an hour away, where they live. My mam and my sister.<br>Paul reckons they can hopefully get me somewhere close. |
| DAN | What's her name? |
| AVA | Who? |
| DAN | Your sister? |
| | *Beat.* |
| AVA | My mam's name's Claire. |
| DAN | My mam died.<br>I mean she's dead.<br>It's been a while, you know, not like she just did it. Died. She died a while ago.<br>Three years. |
| AVA | I didn't know that. |
| DAN | An hour away, you said. |

AVA        I won't come back here. You won't be 'just
           passing' me again.

DAN        I'm not... I wasn't... I was walking by.
           It's not why you think.
           It's not about, you know, that. Although, you
           know, if it, if that, was on offer – I didn't mean on
           offer because I felt bad you know, I don't think
           you should. Offer. Like that, you know I've got a
           sister and so I think about girls, from their point of
           view, feminist, not in that way, not always, but...

           *Breathes.*

           I was on the bus and I was going. I was with
           Marnie. We've been. She's, you know... Me and
           her have been seeing each other. Six months. And
           we was going into town.
           On the bus.
           And she was talking on about shit and her phone
           was buzzing and I was sat leaning against the
           window and I had a thought.
           I thought about that I liked being on the bus and
           looking down at the cars. I thought of you. I
           thought, fuck it she's right. It is good being high
           up. Higher than, you know.

           Marnie was talking on and I was watching her
           mouth and then she starts telling me about a dream
           she had and how mad it was and I thought how
           fucking boring other people's dreams are and the
           words went on and on.
           And I said to her, I said, 'Can I be honest, Marnie,'
           and she says 'Honesty, Dan' and her phone is
           buzzing on, 'Honesty, is overrated.' And then she
           puts her hand on my mouth and answers her phone,
           'Yeah, babes, OM fucking G, Michaela, you are
           shitting me...'

           I got off the bus.
           And I stands at the side of the road looking up at

her as the bus pulls off.
She didn't notice.

AVA     And you came here.

DAN     I was going home.

AVA     But you came here.

DAN     Sometimes I don't know what's at home.
It's still shit, you know. My dad still cries an'…
She had a heart attack. A condition. They thought
she must have had it all her life but she didn't
know. I think it's good that she didn't know. No,
fuck that. I think it's shit that she didn't know
because if she'd known she might still be here.
Anyway, she's not.
She had this thing, you know, about kindness.
About acting with kindness. Treating people right.
And I didn't. I didn't treat you right. So.
I was walking past and I saw you.

*Beat.*

And I came here.
Because.
And bear with me cos I haven't thought this
through. I came here because. I wanted to tell you
about the fishing. I wanted to tell you what I was
thinking.
And before you think anything then don't because
I'm not even sure if I mean it or where it's come
from but I came here because it's in my head.
And not just because, you know, with my dick and
stuff. Fuck it.
I came here because I like you.
There. Said it.
I like you.

AVA *giggles.*

And not because of the… you know.

AVA *giggles*.

I'm gonna learn how to fish.
You can come down the coast with me and me dad.
Or I'll teach ya.

*Beat.*

If you wants to that is.

*The giggles turn into laughing which slowly turn into sobbing.*

DAN *makes his way cautiously to her, puts his arm around her and holds her as she sobs.*

DAN *leaves* AVA *go as* TASH *takes his place.*

AVA *wipes her eyes but stays in hold with* TASH.

TASH    Make a wish.

AVA     Is that you, Tash?

TASH    A birthday wish.

AVA     I can't.

TASH    I wish.

AVA     I wish /

TASH    Close your eyes.

        AVA *closes her eyes.*

        TASH *spins her around.*

        Did I tell you about the bird in a cage, Ava?

AVA     In your nana's lodgings?

TASH    They let me visit me nana for a bit.

AVA     There was a bird. In a cage.

TASH    Mrs Reagan, it was her bird.
        And sometimes she'd let it fly around the room,
        'Look at his face,' she'd say, 'you watch him, you
        watch his face.'

Then she'd open the door on the cage.
'There's sheer joy on that bird's face,' she'd say,
'Look at him, if a bird could laugh with joy that's
what he'd be doing, right now.'

AVA          It was the saddest that bird ever looked.

TASH         Looking at that open cage door.

Showing him how wonderful it was to fly and then
giving him a room ten-foot square to do it in.
I sometimes wonders about me nana.
She might be dead.
I reckon she must be dead.
I hope she's dead.

*AVA giggles.*

Are you laughing about me dead nana, you?

AVA          I am, yeah.

*AVA giggles again.*

*Pushes playfully against TASH.*

*Hold on.*

*Hold her.*

*Hold on to her.*

TASH         I opened the window.

*AVA opens her eyes.*

TASH/AVA     Opened the window and the bird flew away.

*AVA turns to face TASH.*

TASH         She found the other world.

Happy birthday, Ava.

*Shadows and birds.*

TASH *is gone.*

LEE          D'you like curry?

AVA     I do.
        I like korma.

LEE     I got korma.
        I thought you'd like korma. Like Tash.
        We can share.
        You won't mind you're like a sparrow.
        Got you chips, Ava.
        I knows what you likes, don't I.

        *They start to eat.*

AVA     I like your shirt.

LEE     Thank you.

AVA     It's like.
        That western stuff.
        Checked like a rodeo.

LEE     Tuck in.

AVA     A cowboy.
        And the boots.
        Are they proper leather them?

LEE     Straight from the arse of a cow.

AVA     Have you got one of them hats an' all.
        Like one of them.
        What they called.

        Cowboy hats.

LEE     Stetson.

AVA     Have you got one of them, Lee, have ya?

        AVA *laughs.*

        *No response from* LEE.

        You likes all the music an' that, all that achy
        breaky heart.
        D'you do line-dancing?
        I bet you do.
        Do you?
        I can see you there.

Up the club with the boots and the hat and the shirt. Bet you used to do it, when it was all the rage. Before. Did you have a life before?

LEE      I had a life.

AVA     What am I talking about. Course you did. You're old. You've had a life. Lives. Who were you? Were you married? Kids? Stepkids? You went to prison. Tash told me. She said you went to prison for six years. That's a long time that is. What's someone got to do, to go down for six years.

LEE      Who is this?

AVA     That's bad. Got to have been something bad.

LEE      Who are you?

AVA     What?

LEE      Sat here. Acting up. I don't know who you are.

AVA     I'm just me.

LEE      You don't seem right.

AVA     I'm right.

LEE      There's a side to you. A tone.

AVA     There's no side to me.

LEE      There's something. Nerves?

AVA     I'm not nervous.

LEE      You seem it.

AVA     No.

*LEE looks at AVA.*

*Looks her over.*

*Takes her in.*

It's my birthday.

LEE      You're still there? At the home?

| | |
|---|---|
| AVA | Yeah. |
| LEE | I like to know where you are. |
| AVA | Paul's trying to find me a place. |

*A pause while* LEE *digests this.*

| | |
|---|---|
| LEE | There's peregrines. |
| AVA | What? |
| LEE | Nesting in them houses. |
| AVA | What are peregrines? |
| LEE | Nesting in the roofs. |
| AVA | Are they birds? |
| LEE | Birds of prey.<br>A protected species.<br>They're in them houses across the way.<br>Nesting.<br>I'm checking them.<br>Looking out for them. They had chicks.<br>They can't knock them houses down now.<br>If they stays.<br>It's illegal. |

If any man harmed them, Ava, they'd do time, do
you know that?
If I was to harm those birds I'd be in more trouble
than if I had harmed you.
I'm not saying that's right or wrong.
But it's the way it is.

They'll get rid of them in time because the land is
money, knock them houses down but it's an
inconvenience.
And it'll take time.

*Pause.*

They're empty.

*Pause.*

Someone could live there quite happily, for a time.
For years even.
They're good houses.
And no one would be any the wiser.

AVA     I didn't think you could go in them.

LEE     I go in them all the time to check the birds.
They're just houses. Rooms.
Make a good home for someone.

AVA     For me? Is that what you're saying, Lee.

LEE     If you like. I could set you up there. Make it nice
for you.

AVA     Yes.

LEE     It can be your birthday present. From me to you.
A home.

AVA     I'd like to see the birds.

LEE     Although, it would cost, though.

AVA     Would it?

LEE     It would yeah. Food and keep. You know.

AVA     I don't have any money.

LEE     No. Oh.

AVA     What will I do, Lee?

LEE     Oh. Maybe. I don't know. Maybe.
There's ways isn't there.
We can sort something out, anyways.

AVA     I don't know.

LEE     They are lovely old houses though. Full of
character.
Big old rooms.

AVA     Paul said he's looking at supported
accommodation.

| | |
|---|---|
| LEE | Is he? |
| AVA | He is. Could be far away.<br>That's the thing.<br>And I want to be here. |
| LEE | Oh yes. |
| AVA | Birds of prey, you said? |
| LEE | Beautiful beasts, they are. |
| | Tash liked the birds. She had a room at the top.<br>You can see as far as the eye. |
| | *He stops.* |
| AVA | What? |
| | TASH *in here.* |
| LEE | She said it was like a house she lived in with<br>her nana. |
| AVA | Tash? |
| LEE | Right next to the birds, she was. |
| AVA | Tash came here without me? |
| LEE | She said sometimes, she said, she felt caged in that<br>room, she'd open the windows, let the air in and<br>I'd be closing them behind her. There's no heating. |
| AVA | She never told me. |
| LEE | I'll show you the room. |
| AVA | She had a room? |
| LEE | She did. |
| AVA | Why? |
| | *Nothing.* |
| | She stopped coming home. |
| | *Silence.* |

In those weeks, before.
She stopped coming home.

*Silence.*

She was here.
With you.

*Silence.*

I didn't know. I didn't. I didn't think. I didn't see it.

*Silence.*

Thirteen. She was thirteen.

AVA *sticks the fork she has been eating with in* LEE*'s arm.*

You're a disgusting, fuck.

*Stabbing his arm, again and again.*

I'll rip your fucking throat open.

*Again and again.*

LEE *lets her.*

Tear your fucking cock off.

*Again and again.*

TASH    Can you hear me?

AVA     You fucking animal.

TASH    Can you hear me?

        LEE *takes the pain.*

AVA     I would hate to be you.

        *Beside herself.*

        I would hate to be you.

        AVA *slaps and hits him.*

TASH    Can you hear me, Ava?

        *Stops.*

*Wipes her face, straightens her clothes,*
*stands tall.*

TASH *watches him leave.*

AVA      I can hear you.

TASH     Can you see me?

AVA      I can't see you no more.

TASH     Why won't you see me?

AVA      I looked for you.

TASH     I know.

AVA      I went to the park.
         Down the estuary. By the old fair.
         I went to the coast.
         I didn't go to the houses. I didn't think.

TASH     I wasn't there. I was here. Our place.

AVA      You was with him. You never told me.

TASH     There was birds.

AVA      You went with him to the houses.

TASH     Peregrines.

AVA      He gave you a room.

TASH     I thought we could live there.
         Me and you.

AVA      He showed you the birds.

TASH     I watched them birds for hours.

         I never went too close cos of the chicks, you
         know. The mother knows if the chicks been
         messed with.

         And then on that day one of the chicks was getting
         all full of herself and squawking and getting all
         brave and it falls out of the nest. And I knows I

should leave it, let it fend for itself but I can't so I picks it up and puts it back in, quick as you like before the mother comes back.
When I goes back later, she'd destroyed the nest. All the chicks was dead.

It all got too much, Ava.

TASH *grabs* AVA*'s hands. Pulls her to her feet.*

*They hold hands, spinning together.*

*Looking at each other, spinning together.*

*Birds.*

*They let go of each other.*

CLAIRE *at the café.*

| | |
|---|---|
| AVA | Where is she? |
| CLAIRE | I didn't bring her. |
| AVA | I thought you were. |
| CLAIRE | I don't want to confuse her. |
| AVA | Paul told you. I got rights. Sibling rights. A right to know. |
| CLAIRE | She's two. She doesn't understand. |
| AVA | It's my right to know who's in my family. |
| CLAIRE | I told her about you. But at two... you know, she thinks the rabbit's her sister so. |
| | You have to give me some time. |
| AVA | |
| CLAIRE | I don't want her upset. |
| AVA | I was telling my friend about her. |
| CLAIRE | The one you share a room with? |
| AVA | Tash. |

CLAIRE     Right.

AVA        No. He's called Dan.

CLAIRE     Don't want her life disrupted any more.

AVA        Not Tash.

CLAIRE     I wanna do this right.

AVA        Tash is dead.

           *Silence.*

           She died. Three months ago.

           She killed herself.

           *Takes that in.*

CLAIRE

AVA        She was thirteen.

           It was in the papers.

CLAIRE     I didn't know.

AVA        She flew.

CLAIRE     You say shit like that...

AVA        Shit like what.

CLAIRE     She flew.

AVA        Like a bird.

CLAIRE     And I'm supposed to...

AVA        My best friend died.

CLAIRE     D'you know how fucked up you sound? She flew.

AVA        You're supposed to what?

CLAIRE     Jesus, she's two.

AVA        I don't know her name.

CLAIRE     She's two and I don't want you...

AVA           What?

CLAIRE        I don't want you fucking her up.

AVA           Me?

CLAIRE        Yes, you.

AVA           No.

CLAIRE        You. Messing with her head.

AVA           Not me.

CLAIRE        I have to think of her. I have to.

              AVA *laughs*.

AVA           Fuck you.
              Do you know how that sounds? Talk about me.
              And *you*. You sit there and say that. How fucked
              up is that? Sitting there telling *me* you're thinking
              of *her*.

CLAIRE        I knew you'd do this. Jealousy. That's what this is.

AVA           Jealous. This isn't jealous.

CLAIRE        It's all about you.

AVA           It's about her.
              I have to protect her.
              From you.
              From him.

              *Pause*.

CLAIRE        He's gone.

              *Like a slap to the face*.

AVA           What?

CLAIRE        You heard.

AVA           What d'you mean?

CLAIRE        What d'you think I mean.
              He's gone.

AVA            You'll have him back.

CLAIRE         That first time.
               When he went.
               You.
               It was.
               There was a look.
               I forgot about it but I saw him look at you.
               It wasn't anything... just small, a second. That's
               why I forgot about it. But it was enough to. It got
               in. The look. It got into me but I didn't know it
               had. So I started on at him, you know about
               something – nothing – he'd been coming home
               late, not pulling his weight, drinking too much,
               whatever. And he left
               And I wanted him back.

AVA            You knew.

CLAIRE         No.

AVA            All this time you knew.

CLAIRE         There was a hot day. Last week. We got the pool
               out. And she's there all fat and cute. Her legs. You
               could eat 'em.

               He didn't do nothing. We had a lovely day. He's
               a good dad.

               But I remembered. That second.
               And I couldn't.
               I can't.
               I thought every time.
               Every time he plays with her.
               Looks at her.
               And he's not. I'm not saying that he is. I'm not
               saying that I think he is what you said.
               Because I don't. I can't, Ava. I can't think that.

AVA            What's her name?

CLAIRE         I love her.
               More than anything in the world.

And the thought, got in.
And it's there. And it won't go.
And I can't risk it.
Not with her.

*AVA takes it in. A moment of realisation. Her
mother has looked after her sister.*

AVA        You did the right thing by her.

*AVA and CLAIRE look at each other. Holding
each other's eye.*

*AVA smiles to herself.*

*CLAIRE gets the photo out of her bag and gives it
to AVA, and another.*

CLAIRE     Her name's Sasha.

*AVA smiles.*

*Looks at the photos.*

AVA        Sasha.

           I like it.

CLAIRE     It's Russian.

*AVA smiles.*

AVA        Yeah.

*TASH is laughing on the cliff.*

*She stands at the tip of the cliff, the end of the
earth, breathing it in.*

*Arms outstretched like wings.*

*Breathing.*

*Closes her eyes.*

*Breathes.*

*A rumble of noise begins.*

*Look up.*

*The sky.*

*Noise and movement through the sky.*

*Wonder.*

*Giggling behind her.*

AVA.

*Noise and movement through the sky.*

*Giggling increases.*

TASH *grabs* AVA.

*The swell of noise increases.*

*Movements in the sky, shadows. Birds.*

*Fly over randomly.*

*Increasing in numbers.*

TASH *and* AVA *look at each other.*

*Hold each other's gaze.*

TASH *grabs* AVA*'s hands.*

*They giggle.*

*Hold hands, spinning together.*

*Looking at each other, laughing with each other.*

*Spinning together, they watch the birds with delight, still holding hands.*

*Birds.*

*A deafening surge of migrating birds fly overhead.*

*The most magical theatrical murmuration.*

*Swooping, swirling, whoosing and twirling.*

*Swarming around the girls, a mass of noise and feathers and movement and spectacle, engulfing the girls until they are no longer visible.*

*The birds fly away.*

*AVA is alone, standing at the tip of the cliff, the end of the earth, breathing it in.*

*Arms outstretched like wings.*

*A single bird flies by.*

*AVA smiles.*

*Peace.*

*DAN approaches her, holding two fishing sticks.*

*AVA turns from the cliff edge, laughs and hugs DAN.*

*He picks her up and swings her around.*

*A bird flies past.*

*AVA takes a fishing stick.*

*AVA and DAN stab into the water laughing and playing, messing around.*

*A bird flies past.*

*Fade to black.*

*The End.*

**Other Titles in this Series**

Naylah Ahmed
MUSTAFA

Mike Bartlett
BULL
GAME
AN INTERVENTION
KING CHARLES III
WILD

Jez Butterworth
JERUSALEM
JEZ BUTTERWORTH PLAYS: ONE
MOJO
THE NIGHT HERON
PARLOUR SONG
THE RIVER
THE WINTERLING

Katherine Chandler
BEFORE IT RAINS

Caryl Churchill
BLUE HEART
CHURCHILL PLAYS: THREE
CHURCHILL PLAYS: FOUR
CHURCHILL: SHORTS
CLOUD NINE
DING DONG THE WICKED
A DREAM PLAY
    *after* Strindberg
DRUNK ENOUGH TO SAY
    I LOVE YOU?
ESCAPED ALONE
FAR AWAY
HERE WE GO
HOTEL
ICECREAM
LIGHT SHINING IN
    BUCKINGHAMSHIRE
LOVE AND INFORMATION
MAD FOREST
A NUMBER
SEVEN JEWISH CHILDREN
THE SKRIKER
THIS IS A CHAIR
THYESTES *after* Seneca
TRAPS

Phil Davies
FIREBIRD

Gareth Farr
BRITANNIA WAVES THE RULES
THE QUIET HOUSE

Vivienne Franzmann
MOGADISHU
PESTS
THE WITNESS

debbie tucker green
BORN BAD
DIRTY BUTTERFLY
HANG
NUT
RANDOM
STONING MARY
TRADE & GENERATIONS
TRUTH AND RECONCILIATION

Vicky Jones
THE ONE

Anna Jordan
CHICKEN SHOP
FREAK
YEN

Lucy Kirkwood
BEAUTY AND THE BEAST
    *with* Katie Mitchell
BLOODY WIMMIN
CHIMERICA
HEDDA *after* Ibsen
IT FELT EMPTY WHEN THE
    HEART WENT AT FIRST BUT
    IT IS ALRIGHT NOW
NSFW
TINDERBOX

Laura Lomas
BIRD & OTHER MONOLOGUES FOR
    YOUNG WOMEN

Cordelia Lynn
LELA & CO.

Ben Musgrave
CRUSHED SHELLS AND MUD
PRETEND YOU HAVE BIG
    BUILDINGS

Janice Okoh
EGUSI SOUP
THREE BIRDS

Fiona Peek
SALT

Evan Placey
CONSENSUAL
GIRLS LIKE THAT
GIRLS LIKE THAT & OTHER PLAYS
    FOR TEENAGERS
PRONOUN

James Rushbrooke
TOMCAT

Andrew Sheridan
WINTERLONG

Stef Smith
HUMAN ANIMALS
REMOTE
SWALLOW

Jack Thorne
2ND MAY 1997
BUNNY
BURYING YOUR BROTHER IN
    THE PAVEMENT
HOPE
JACK THORNE PLAYS: ONE
LET THE RIGHT ONE IN
    *after* John Ajvide Lindqvist
MYDIDAE
THE SOLID LIFE OF SUGAR WATER
STACY & FANNY AND FAGGOT
WHEN YOU CURE ME

Phoebe Waller-Bridge
FLEABAG

**A Nick Hern Book**

*Bird* first published in Great Britain in 2016 as a paperback original by Nick Hern Books Limited, The Glasshouse, 49a Goldhawk Road, London W12 8QP, in association with Sherman Cymru, Cardiff, and the Royal Exchange Theatre, Manchester

Cover image: Burning Red

Designed and typeset by Nick Hern Books, London
Printed in the UK by Mimeo Ltd, Huntingdon, Cambridgeshire PE29 6XX

A CIP catalogue record for this book is available from the British Library

ISBN 978 1 84842 565 1